Jumpstarters for U.S. Government

Short Daily Warm-ups for the Classroom

By
TEDDY MEISTER

COPYRIGHT © 2008 Mark Twain Media, Inc.

ISBN 978-1-58037-474-3

Printing No. CD-404099

Mark Twain Media, Inc., Publishers
Distributed by Carson-Dellosa Publishing LLC

Visit us at www.carsondellosa.com

Table of Contents

Introduction to the Teacher

Jumpstarters for U.S. Government provides daily reviews for skills previously learned by students as they prepare for the day's lessons. Each page contains five warm-ups, one for each day of the school week. Students will use problem-solving skills as they compare and contrast, analyze issues, and gain additional insights into our government.

Suggestions for using warm-up activities:

- Copy and cut apart one page each week. Give students one warm-up activity each day at the beginning of class.

- Give each student a copy of the entire page to keep in their binders to complete as assigned.

- Make transparencies of individual warms-ups and complete activities as a group.

- Put copies of warm-ups in a learning center for students to complete on their own when they have a few extra minutes.

- Use warm-ups as homework assignments.

- Use warm-ups as questions in a review game.

- Keep some warm-ups on hand to use when the class has a few extra minutes before dismissal.

The American's Creed

I believe in the United States of America as a Government of the people, by the people, for the people; whose just powers are derived from the consent of the governed; a democracy in a republic; a sovereign Nation of many sovereign states; a perfect union, one and inseparable; established upon those principles of freedom, equality, justice, and humanity for which American patriots sacrificed their lives and fortunes.

I therefore believe it is my duty to my Country to love it; to support its Constitution; to obey its laws; to respect its flag; and to defend it against all enemies.

– William Tyler Page, 1917

U.S. Government Warm-ups: The Mayflower Compact

Name/Date _____

The Mayflower Compact 1

In a ship about the size of a basketball court, 102 Pilgrims spent weeks crossing the Atlantic Ocean. Blown off course, the ship finally neared land. Even though winter was coming soon, the Pilgrim leaders insisted on agreeing to a form of government for the colony before they left the ship. Imagine you were on that journey. Write your thoughts about the experience on your own paper.

"We can't survive in this New World until we can get along with each other."
– William Bradford, author of the Mayflower Compact

Name/Date _____

The Mayflower Compact 2

Before going ashore (November 11, 1620), the Mayflower Compact was written and signed. It later became the basis of government in the New World. Identify a main idea from the Mayflower Compact.

_____
_____
_____

Name/Date _____

The Mayflower Compact 3

Circle the incorrect word in the sentence below.

Eventually, the Pilgrims

could fulfill their own

needs by fishing, farming,

trading, and hunting.

Name/Date _____

The Mayflower Compact 4

The Mayflower Compact is thought of as the foundation for which two major documents of our government?

_____
_____
_____

Name/Date _____

The Mayflower Compact 5

Read the Mayflower Compact. Use "Mayflower Compact" as the keyword to search for the document online. State the overall theme on your own paper. (You may do this at home or on an available school computer when you have time.)

Mayflower Compact
In ye name of God Amen.- The whole names are underwritten

U.S. Government Warm-ups: Colonial Government

Name/Date _____

Colonial Government 1

Fill in the blanks.

In 1619, the house of _____

was formed in _____,

Virginia. Members were chosen by the

_____ .

Name/Date _____

Colonial Government 2

What caused Bacon's Rebellion? Write your answer on your own paper.

Name/Date _____

Colonial Government 3

The following statements are about opinions in the colonies just before the American Revolution. Mark "T" for true and "F" for false.

> "The best ideas are common property."
> – Seneca

1. _____ Other colonies were interested in the same freedoms as Virginia.

2. _____ Some of the colonies were still loyal to King George.

3. _____ Many colonies wanted to keep their British governors.

Name/Date _____

Colonial Government 4

Europeans came to America to experience freedoms they could not in their home countries. On your own paper, list two freedoms each found in the Rhode Island colony, the New Jersey colony, and the Pennsylvania colony.

RI

NJ

Name/Date _____

Colonial Government 5

State a major way the 13 colonies and the United States today are alike.

_____

_____

_____

_____

_____

_____

U.S. Government Warm-ups: Declaration of Independence

Name/Date _____

Declaration of Independence 1

Seeking independence from England, the representatives of the thirteen colonies wrote and signed a declaration of independence. Fill in the blanks of the opening statement of the declaration.

"When in the course of human _____ it

becomes necessary for one _____ to

dissolve the _____ bonds which have

_____ them with one another."

Name/Date _____

Declaration of Independence 2

Examine the Declaration of Independence and list any five members who signed it.

1. _____
2. _____
3. _____
4. _____
5. _____

Name/Date _____

Declaration of Independence 3

Thomas Jefferson was the major author of this document. Pretend that he visited your classroom today. What technologies that writers use today would surprise him?

_____

_____

_____

_____

Name/Date _____

Declaration of Independence 4

What is the official date the Declaration was adopted?

_____

> *This is a world of action, and not for moping and droning in.*
> *– Charles Dickens*

Name/Date _____

Declaration of Independence 5

What signer from Virginia motivated the writing of the Declaration by stating: "That these united colonies are, and of right ought to be, free and independent states…"

_____

_____

U.S. Government Warm-ups:
Declaration of Independence (cont.)

Name/Date _____

Declaration of Independence 6

If the colonies had lost the war for independence, the signers of the Declaration of Independence could have been tried for treason against England. Use a dictionary to define treason.

_____

_____

_____

Name/Date _____

Declaration of Independence 7

Hearing about the Declaration of Independence, many colonists were distressed, especially the Loyalists. Who were they?

_____

_____

_____

_____

Name/Date _____

Declaration of Independence 8

The Declaration of Independence includes a statement of basic human rights that begins: "We hold these truths to be self-evident…" Complete the phrase on your own paper.

Name/Date _____

Declaration of Independence 9

Explain the phrase, "these rights are unalienable."

_____

_____

_____

_____

Name/Date _____

Declaration of Independence 10

A long list of human rights abuses by the King were written into the Declaration. List any three.

1. _____

2. _____

3. _____

U.S. Government Warm-ups: The Constitution

Name/Date _____

The Constitution 1

Fill in the blanks.

In 1787, the Constitutional Convention was held in _____ at Independence Hall. _____ _____ was selected as president of the convention by the delegates attending.

Name/Date _____

The Constitution 2

James Wilson stated, "We are providing a constitution for future generations and not merely for the peculiar circumstances of the moment."

James Wilson was a delegate from

_____.

Name/Date _____

The Constitution 3

After a review of the Constitution, delegates wanted to add a statement of "the fundamental rights of the people that could not be interfered with." What was added after the Constitution was ratified?

_____

Name/Date _____

The Constitution 4

Select any one of the following known figures of the time. Write a brief biographical paragraph about him.

Benjamin Franklin
John Jay
Rufus King
James Madison

Name/Date _____

The Constitution 5

> "The final test of a leader is that he leaves behind him in other men the conviction and the will to carry on."
> – Walter Lippmann

Think about the above quote. List five qualities a good leader should have. Create a small poster on art paper illustrating these qualities.

U.S. Government Warm-ups: The Constitution (cont.)

Name/Date _____

The Constitution 6

Memorize and recite the Preamble to the Constitution.

We the People of the United States, in order to form a more perfect union, establish justice, insure domestic tranquility, provide for the common defense, promote the general welfare, and secure the blessings of liberty to ourselves and our posterity, do ordain and establish this Constitution for the United States of America.

Name/Date _____

The Constitution 7

Use a dictionary to define tranquility, posterity, and domestic. Use your own paper.

Name/Date _____

The Constitution 8

Colonial leaders wanted a Constitution that would outline the powers and responsibilities of the federal and state governments.

Describe one document in your school that outlines what students do. It might be a dress code or the policy for student absences, office referrals, or the grading system. Use your own paper.

Name/Date _____

The Constitution 9

All public officials must take an oath to support the Constitution. Write a short "oath" of office for a club or group in your school.

_____

_____

_____

_____

Name/Date _____

The Constitution 10

Why is the Constitution often referred to as a "living" document?

_____

_____

_____

_____

U.S. Government Warm-ups:
The Bill of Rights

Name/Date _____

The Bill of Rights 1

Fill in the blanks.

What you cannot enforce do not command.
— Sophocles

The Bill of Rights was added to the _____ in _____. It is the first

10 _____ to that document.

Name/Date _____

The Bill of Rights 2

Circle the rights that make the statement correct.

Freedom of Speech

Amendment 1 guarantees freedom of speech, freedom of religion, the right to carry weapons, the right to assemble, the right to vote, freedom of the press, the right to petition, and the right to hold elections.

Name/Date _____

The Bill of Rights 3

What does Amendment 6 say about criminal prosecutions? _____

_____

_____

_____

Name/Date _____

The Bill of Rights 4

Sometimes the media are criticized for their zealous use of freedom of the press.

Do you agree or disagree that freedom of the press is a good idea? Why? _____

_____

Name/Date _____

The Bill of Rights 5

Why have the Constitution and the Bill of Rights lasted so long? _____

_____

_____

U.S. Government Warm-ups: The Bill of Rights (cont.)

Name/Date _____

The Bill of Rights 6

Explain the meaning of "due process" mentioned in Amendment 5. Use your own paper.

Name/Date _____

The Bill of Rights 7

We have many rights in this country and we must not abuse them. Individual rights carry a lot of _____ for citizens.

Name/Date _____

The Bill of Rights 8

Answer "Y" for yes and "N" for no for each situation.

_____ 1. My personal property is safe, but I can be searched at any time.
_____ 2. If I have a problem, I can say whatever I want about it.
_____ 3. A group of my friends or peers can decide if I do something wrong.
_____ 4. Weapons in school are forbidden.
_____ 5. The local government wants private citizens to house and feed soldiers. Should they do that?

Name/Date _____

The Bill of Rights 9

Which amendment is the most important one for you? Why?

_____

_____

_____

_____

Name/Date _____

The Bill of Rights 10

Match the term to the amendment in which it is found.

_____ 1. double jeopardy   a. 5
_____ 2. bear arms   b. 8
_____ 3. quartering soldiers   c. 2
_____ 4. excessive bail   d. 3

U.S. Government Warm-ups: A Bill Becomes a Law

How a Bill Becomes a Law

Begins in Senate ⟶ Review, research, discuss ⟶ Vote to adopt or reject ⟶ Members of the House review and discuss ⟶ Vote to adopt or reject ⟶ When accepted by both houses and signed by the president, it becomes a law ⟶ If vetoed by the president, it goes back to Congress ⟶ If two-thirds majority of both the House and Senate vote to override the presidential veto, the bill becomes a law.

Name/Date _____

A Bill Becomes a Law 1

Subcommittees recommend bills for passage by the House and Senate. Which subcommittees are your representatives and senators on?

_____
_____
_____
_____

Name/Date _____

A Bill Becomes a Law 2

Using the internet, look up a bill that was recently passed by Congress. How did your representatives and senators vote on it? Did you agree or disagree with their votes? Write your response on your own paper.

Name/Date _____

A Bill Becomes a Law 3

1. How many votes must a bill get in the Senate to pass? _____
2. How many votes must a bill get in the House to pass? _____
3. How many votes must a bill get in the Senate to be veto-proof? _____
4. How many votes must a bill get in the House to be veto-proof? _____

Name/Date _____

A Bill Becomes a Law 4

Which house of Congress is the only one who can introduce tax bills? Why?

_____
_____
_____

Name/Date _____

A Bill Becomes a Law 5

What is a pocket veto?

_____
_____
_____
_____

U.S. Government Warm-ups: Native Americans

Name/Date _____

Native Americans 1

The Indian Reorganization Act of 1934 attempted to reverse the harm done to tribal cultures by the U.S. government policies of the past. Research this act and write "Y" for yes and "N" for no beside each statement.

_____ 1. Native Americans could organize their own tribal governments.

_____ 2. Loans were made available for tuition to colleges and trade schools.

_____ 3. Reservation dwellers had to pay taxes to the government.

_____ 4. Loans could be made to Native American corporations.

_____ 5. Mining could not occur on reservations.

Name/Date _____

Native Americans 2

This Native American group had a form of government, complete with a constitution, that effectively managed conflicting interests of different tribes. What was this governing body called?

_____

Name/Date _____

Native Americans 3

What government organization is in charge of managing Native American issues? List two things that organization does.

_____

_____

_____

_____

Name/Date _____

Native Americans 4

The Navajo Nation covers parts of Arizona, New Mexico, Utah, and Colorado. List three ways their government is similar to the United States government.

_____

_____

_____

Name/Date _____

Native Americans 5

Who is Ben Nighthorse Campbell? What high ranking did he achieve in the U.S. government?

_____

_____

U.S. Government Warm-ups: Statehood

Name/Date _____

Statehood 1

Fill in the blanks.

Congress presented its plans for governing the _____ lands under the _____ _____ of 1787. This provided guidelines for territories to become _____.

Name/Date _____

Statehood 2

Circle the words that make the statement true.

The Northwest Ordinance of (1767 / 1787) promotes (self-government / free speech).

> *The man who goes alone can start today; but he who travels with another must wait till that other is ready.*
>
> *– Henry David Thoreau*

Name/Date _____

Statehood 3

Circle the correct word.

The Northwest Ordinance provided for the founding of (newspapers / schools) in new areas and proclaimed that slavery (would / would not) be permitted.

Name/Date _____

Statehood 4

There were three stages in the process to become a state. Check the one that is NOT one of the stages.

_____ 1. population of 5,000 adult males

_____ 2. have a lawmaking body

_____ 3. 100 towns were settled

_____ 4. total population reached 60,000

Name/Date _____

Statehood 5

Every state has a motto and a flag that reflect the philosophy of that state. What does your state's motto and flag say about your state?

_____

_____

_____

_____

U.S. Government Warm-ups: Statehood (cont.)

Name/Date _____

Statehood 6

List four current U.S. Territories

1. _____

2. _____

3. _____

4. _____

Name/Date _____

Statehood 7

Which two states were once independent countries? When did they join the United States?

1. _____

2. _____

Name/Date _____

Statehood 8

When did your state officially join the United States? If you live in a southern state, when did your state re-join the United States after the Civil War?

_____

_____

_____

Name/Date _____

Statehood 9

Which state split into two states during the Civil War? What was the new state called?

_____

_____

Name/Date _____

Statehood 10

Fill in the blanks.

After World War II, Alaska and Hawaii became states. They were the _____ and _____ states to join the United States.

U.S. Government Warm-ups: State and Local Governments

Name/Date _____

State and Local Governments 1

Circle the powers Amendment 10 of the Bill of Rights gave to state governments.

FAMILY BILL OF RIGHTS

1. education
2. family law
3. contract law
4. jurisdiction over most crimes
5. all of the above

Name/Date _____

State and Local Governments 2

Fill in the blanks.

State governments have _____ branches,

which are the _____,

_____, and

_____.

Name/Date _____

State and Local Governments 3

Fill in the blanks.

The chief executive of a state is called the

_____. He or she is

responsible for developing a _____,

which directs how the state will spend its money.

Who is the chief executive of your state? _____

> *Opinions cannot survive if one has no chance to fight for them.*
> *– Thomas Mann*

Name/Date _____

State and Local Governments 4

Circle the document that originally provided the states with powers.

1. Bill of Rights
2. Declaration of Independence
3. Constitution
4. all of the above
5. none of the above

Name/Date _____

State and Local Governments 5

Why don't you need a passport to visit other states? How would life be different if every state required a passport to enter?

_____

_____

_____

U.S. Government Warm-ups: State and Local Governments (cont.)

Name/Date _____

_____

State and Local Governments 6

Circle the areas below over which local governments have power.

1. fire and police protection

2. sanitary and health regulations

3. public transportation

4. all of the above

5. none of the above

Name/Date _____

State and Local Governments 7

Circle the divisions of local governments.

1. county
2. municipalities
3. special districts
4. all of the above
5. none of the above

Name/Date _____

State and Local Governments 8

Units of local government were created and set up by the colonies. How did this help unite the country?

_____

_____

Name/Date _____

State and Local Governments 9

Local governments are run in many ways. Who is in charge of the government in your area? What is that person's name?

_____

_____

Name/Date _____

State and Local Governments 10

On your own paper, draw a labeled diagram showing the organization of your school. How is it similar to how your local government is organized?

U.S. Government Warm-ups: State and Local Governments (cont.)

Name/Date _____

State and Local Governments 11

City governments vary widely. Most have an elected central group. This consists of a main officer and department heads in charge of city business. Write a two-sentence description of your local city government.

_____

_____

_____

Name/Date _____

State and Local Governments 12

A county or parish is a portion of a state. What is the name of your county or parish?

_____

Name/Date _____

State and Local Governments 13

Most counties have a county seat where government offices are located and supervisory committees meet. Where is your county seat located? Do you think that is the best location?

_____

_____

_____

Name/Date _____

State and Local Governments 14

An elected board governs smaller towns. Underline the functions of an elected board.

1. clerk
2. treasurer
3. sanitation control
4. police and fire services
5. health services
6. public relations

Name/Date _____

State and Local Governments 15

Town meetings allow voters to attend and have a say in issues concerning them. Is this good or bad? Why? Write your answer on your own paper.

U.S. Government Warm-ups:
State and Local Governments (cont.)

Name/Date _____

State and Local Governments 16

Using the list of Federal, State, and Local Governments Job Roles, identify the job roles at the local government level.

_____

_____

_____

Federal, State, and Local Governments Job Roles

IRS	highway patrol
police	forest ranger
fire marshal	Dept. of Motor Vehicles
health inspector	Dept. of Agriculture
FBI	Food and Drug
fire chief	Administration

Name/Date _____

State and Local Governments 17

Using the list of Federal, State, and Local Governments Job Roles, identify the job roles at the state government level.

_____

_____

_____

Name/Date _____

State and Local Governments 18

Using the list of Federal, State, and Local Governments Job Roles, identify the job roles at the national government level.

_____

_____

_____

Name/Date _____

State and Local Governments 19

The number to call for help in emergencies is

_____.

Name/Date _____

State and Local Governments 20

Many schools have a safety officer on campus. Talk to one and find out what his or her job role involves.

_____

_____

_____

U.S. Government Warm-ups: Women in Government

Name/Date _____

Women in Government 1

Sandra Day O'Conner was the first woman to serve as a Supreme Court Justice.

Who was the second female justice to serve on the Supreme Court?_____

Name/Date _____

Women in Government 2

Mary Edwards Walker (1832–1919) was a surgeon with the Union Army and a prisoner of war during the Civil War. She was the first woman to receive the highest medal in the land. What is the name of the medal Walker received?

_____

Name/Date _____

Women in Government 3

Clare Boothe Luce (1903–1987) was a United States Congresswoman and ambassador.

What European country was Luce appointed to?

_____

Name/Date _____

Women in Government 4

Carrie Chapman Catt (1859–1947) was the founder of the League of Women Voters.

On your own paper, write a short paragraph about the merits of women serving in government roles.

Name/Date _____

_____

Women in Government 5

Select one of the women listed below who have held U.S. Cabinet positions and list the title of the position she held.

1. Frances Perkins
2. Oveta Culp Hobby
3. Patricia Harris
4. Elizabeth Dole
5. Hazel O'Leary
6. Janet Reno
7. Madeleine Albright
8. Condoleezza Rice
9. Elaine Chao

U.S. Government Warm-ups: Women in Government (cont.)

Name/Date _____

Women in Government 6

Write one sentence describing the role in history of each of the following women.

1. Dorothea Dix (1802–1887) _____
_____

2. Clara Barton (1821–1912) _____
_____

3. Lucretia Mott (1793–1880) _____
_____

Name/Date _____

Women in Government 7

What do you think was the view of society about the role of women in government at the turn of the century?

_____
_____
_____

Name/Date _____

Women in Government 8

Unscramble the name of the woman who campaigned for a law against the sale and public use of alcoholic beverages.

I R A C R E   A N N I T O

_____

Name/Date _____

Women in Government 9

Unscramble the name of this famous First Lady who later became an ambassador to the United Nations.

N L O E A E R
R E S O V O T E L

_____

Name/Date _____

Women in Government 10

List three interesting facts about your favorite First Lady.

_____
_____
_____

U.S. Government Warm-ups: Minorities in Government

Name/Date _____

_____

Minorities in Government 1

Name the people who were first in each category below.

1. African-American in the Senate:

   _____

2. Woman in the House of Representatives:

   _____

3. African-American woman in the House of Representatives:

   _____

4. Japanese-American in the Senate:

   _____

5. African-American on the Supreme Court:

   _____

6. African-American woman in the Senate:

   _____

7. Hispanic-American Governor:

   _____

Name/Date _____

Minorities in Government 2

Who was the first African-American to be the chairman of the Joint Chiefs of Staff and the Secretary of State?

_____

Name/Date _____

Minorities in Government 3

In 2008, for the first time, a woman and an African-American were the front-runners to be the Democratic candidate for president. Name these two senators.

_____

Name/Date _____

Minorities in Government 4

This African-American woman has been the provost of Stanford University, the National Security Advisor to President George W. Bush, and the Secretary of State.

Who is she? _____

Name/Date _____

Minorities in Government 5

Antonia Coello was appointed to a position in George H.W. Bush's administration. She was the first woman and the first Hispanic to hold this position.

What was her job title? _____

U.S. Government Warm-ups: Government Agencies

Name/Date _____

Government Agencies 1

The Environmental Protection Agency (EPA) is charged with safeguarding air, water, and land. List three issues this agency addresses.

_____

_____

_____

Name/Date _____

Government Agencies 2

What is the role of the Food and Drug Administration (FDA)?

_____

_____

_____

Name/Date _____

Government Agencies 3

The Central Intelligence Agency (CIA) collects and analyzes political, economic, and military information from around the world. Where is the CIA's main location?

_____

> To see the vast number of other government agencies, do a keyword search for "Government Agencies."

Name/Date _____

Government Agencies 4

The Federal Bureau of Investigation (FBI) tracks crime alerts, fugitives, and terrorists. List three requirements for becoming an agent.

_____

_____

_____

_____

Name/Date _____

Government Agencies 5

The Internal Revenue Service (IRS) is responsible for tax collection and tax law enforcement. What government department oversees this agency?

_____

U.S. Government Warm-ups: Government Agencies (cont.)

Name/Date _____

Government Agencies 6

The Department of Veterans Affairs (VA) administers benefits and services for veterans of the U.S. military, their children, and their widows or widowers. Read the quote by Abraham Lincoln and then fill in the blanks.

> *Let us strive on to finish the work we are in. . . . to care for him who shall have borne the battle and for his widow and his orphan.*
> *– Abraham Lincoln*

Lincoln pledged the government's obligation to care for the

_____ and aid the _____

of those who had died.

Name/Date _____

Government Agencies 7

The Department of Homeland Security has the responsibility to "protect the United States from hazards inside and outside the country, natural or man-made." Explain what "natural or man-made" means.

_____

_____

Name/Date _____

Government Agencies 8

The Federal Emergency Management Agency (FEMA) works to reduce the loss of life and property during an emergency. Circle the following things that do not qualify as an emergency.

1. acts of terrorism   2. crime

3. natural disaster   4. property lawsuits

5. power blackout   6. car accidents

Name/Date _____

Government Agencies 9

The Drug Enforcement Agency (DEA) works to prevent drug trafficking and abuse. What are some ways the DEA fights to keep America safe?

_____

_____

_____

Name/Date _____

Government Agencies 10

The Federal Trade Commission (FTC) monitors goods traded within and outside the country. Why is it important to have this government service?

_____

_____

_____

U.S. Government Warm-ups: Military Branches of the Government

Name/Date _____

Military Branches of the Government 1

Answer the following questions about the United States military. Use the Internet or other sources to help you.

> *The purpose of freedom is to create it for others.*
> *– Bernard Malamud*

1. How many men and women are enlisted in the Army? _____
2. Who is the Commander in Chief? _____
3. What Cabinet position is responsible for the entire military? _____
4. What are the five branches of the military? _____,
   _____, _____,
   _____, _____

Name/Date _____

Military Branches of the Government 2

Write "T" for true and "F" for false.

_____ 1. The U.S. has a volunteer military.
_____ 2. The Coast Guard is separate from the Navy.
_____ 3. Women can serve in all combat areas.
_____ 4. The eligible age for joining the military is 21 to 60.

Name/Date _____

Military Branches of the Government 3

In 1775, the first Continental Congress formed the Army for what purpose?

_____

_____

_____

Name/Date _____

Military Branches of the Government 4

What are the qualifications for joining the ROTC? What does the ROTC do? Write your answer on your own paper.

Name/Date _____

Military Branches of the Government 5

The three major medals awarded to servicemen and women are the Medal of Honor, the Distinguished Service Cross, and the Silver Star. What is each medal awarded for?

_____

_____

_____

U.S. Government Warm-ups: The United States Mint

Name/Date _____

The United States Mint 1

What is the name of the Act passed by Congress in 1792 that created the United States Mint?

The _____ Act

Name/Date _____

The United States Mint 2

What are the six denominations, or amounts, of coins minted in the United States for everyday use?

1. _____   2. _____
3. _____   4. _____
5. _____   6. _____

Name/Date _____

The United States Mint 3

Where are the facilities located for making and regulating money?

1. _____

2. _____

Do what you can, with what you have, where you are.
– Theodore Roosevelt

Name/Date _____

The United States Mint 4

Using the financial section of the newspaper, track the price of gold for five days. Then compute the average price for the week.

Name/Date _____

The United States Mint 5

Coin collecting is a great hobby. Write to the American Numismatic Society; 96 Fulton St.; New York, NY 10038 for free information.

U.S. Government Warm-ups: Immigration

Name/Date _____

Immigration 1

Read the clues and name this historic site.

For decades, millions of immigrants came here first. I am located in upper New York Bay. With the "lady" standing next to me, I am a national monument.

Who am I? _____

Name/Date _____

Immigration 2

Fill in the blanks with letters that match the words from the list.

a) board of inquiry
b) legal inspectors
c) background checks
d) medical exams
e) detained

As immigrants arrived, they were given _____, _____, and had to wait for _____. If they were not approved, they could be _____ to appear before a _____.

Name/Date _____

Immigration 3

Circle the correct words.

By the late (1800s / 1900s), as immigration (decreased / increased), social and economic forces (added / closed) the "open door policy."

Name/Date _____

Immigration 4

During World War I, Congress passed laws limiting immigration to about 150,000 people a year. How did that change with the Johnson-Reed Act of 1924?

_____

_____

_____

Name/Date _____

Immigration 5

Nearly every immigration law deals with quotas for immigrants. What is a quota?

_____

_____

U.S. Government Warm-ups:
Immigration (cont.)

Name/Date _____

Immigration 6

There are two kinds of immigrants: legal and illegal. Write definitions for each.

legal: _____
_____

illegal: _____
_____

Name/Date _____

Immigration 7

What government agency is charged with overseeing immigration to America?

_____

Name/Date _____

Immigration 8

People come to the United States for many different reasons. List three reasons someone would immigrate to the United States.

_____
_____
_____

Name/Date _____

Immigration 9

What is naturalization?

_____
_____
_____

Name/Date _____
_____

Immigration 10

Answer the following questions on your own paper.

1. Where were typical immigrants from in the late 1800s to the early 1900s?

2. Where are typical immigrants from today?

3. Why do you think it changed?

U.S. Government Warm-ups: Immigration (cont.)

Name/Date _____

Immigration 11

Foreigners who come to America need a passport and a visa.

What is a passport? _____
_____

What is a visa? _____
_____
_____

Name/Date _____

Immigration 12

Which two islands were historically the centers of immigration on the east and west coasts?

1. _____

2. _____

Name/Date _____

Immigration 13

If your parents are American citizens, but you are born in Spain, are you an American citizen? What is your official citizenship title?

_____
_____
_____

Name/Date _____

Immigration 14

List three famous people who are naturalized American citizens.

1. _____

2. _____

3. _____

Name/Date _____

Immigration 15

Write a short paragraph stating how you think current immigration has impacted our country.

_____
_____
_____
_____
_____

U.S. Government Warm-ups: The U.S. National Archives & Records Administration

---

Name/Date _____

The NARA 1

Use a dictionary to define *archive*.

_____

_____

_____

ARCHIVE

Name/Date _____

The NARA 2

Fill in the blanks with words from the box.

U.S. Government Congress documents

Established by _____

in 1934, the NARA keeps forever all important

_____ and materials

relating to the _____.

Name/Date _____

The NARA 3

Unscramble the words relating to the original copies held by the NARA.

1. E C D R L A T A I O N F O P D I N E E C K N E N E

   _____

2. L I L B F O I G R T H S _____

3. I M N E A T A C I P O N R O M P C L A T I A O N

   _____

4. O N U T C S I T T O N I _____

> *We can lick gravity, but sometimes the paperwork is overwhelming.*
> – Wernher von Baun

Name/Date _____

The NARA 4

Mark "Y" for yes and "N" for no to identify the kinds of documents the NARA keeps.

1. family histories _____
2. government positions _____
3. research _____
4. the national system of libraries _____
5. medical research _____

Name/Date _____

The NARA 5

Documents archived by the NARA are part of the public domain. What does that mean?

_____

_____

_____

The National Archives

U.S. Government Warm-ups: The Census Bureau

Name/Date _____

The Census Bureau 1

Fill in the blanks with words from the box.

The _____ requires a census

taken every _____ years to determine the

number of _____ each

_____ can have. The next census will be held in

_____.

> *He who knows only his own side of the case knows little of that.*
> *– John Stuart Mill*

| U.S. Constitution |
| 2010 |
| representatives |
| ten |
| state |

Name/Date _____

The Census Bureau 2

Use a dictionary to define decennial.

_____

_____

_____

Decennial

Name/Date _____

The Census Bureau 3

Write "Y" for yes and "N" for no.

_____ 1. The census is printed in six languages.

_____ 2. The first census was taken in 1850.

_____ 3. It took 18 months to count 3.9 million people in the first census.

_____ 4. Between 1790 and 1840, the number of census questions rose from 6 to 30.

Name/Date _____

The Census Bureau 4

Unscramble these three areas that receive federal monies based on census numbers.

1. S O C H O L S

_____

2. N T N S R A P O A T R T I O

_____

3. L C I A S O   V R I C S E S E

_____

Name/Date _____

The Census Bureau 5

Do you think the census is important? Why or why not? Write a paragraph on your own paper.

U.S. Government Warm-ups:
The Electoral College

Name/Date _____

The Electoral College 1

Mark "T" for true and "F" for false.

_____ 1. Primary elections are part of the process to determine a party's candidate.

_____ 2. A voter can register as a member of one party but vote for another in the general election.

_____ 3. Changing political parties carries penalties.

Name/Date _____

The Electoral College 2

Using your own paper, write a definition of the Electoral College.

> *One of the best ways to persuade others is with your ears—by listening to them.*
>
> *– Dean Rusk*

Name/Date _____

The Electoral College 3

The Electoral College process provides fair representation of votes for each state. What majority is needed to elect the President?

_____

_____

Name/Date _____

The Electoral College 4

Circle those that cannot be appointed to the Electoral College.

1. Senators   2. Governors

3. Mayors   4. Representatives

5. Presidents

Name/Date _____

The Electoral College 5

How is the total number of electors determined?

_____

_____

_____

U.S. Government Warm-ups: Elections

Name/Date _____

Elections 1

Fill in the blanks.

When people go to the _____ place, they vote for _____ chosen by the political parties. A majority in the _____ college will determine the new president and vice president.

Name/Date _____

Elections 2

Four amendments deal with voting rights: the 15th, 19th, 24th, and 26th. Choose one and summarize it in one sentence below.

_____
_____
_____

Name/Date _____

Elections 3

Place a check mark next to the people who are eligible to vote in a national election.

_____ 1. A 19-year-old American girl

_____ 2. A 17-year-old American boy

_____ 3. A 79-year-old African-American man

_____ 4. A 25-year-old resident alien

_____ 5. A 50-year-old Asian-American woman

Name/Date _____

Elections 4

If there was an election for school president, list three qualifications the candidates would need to have.

1. _____

2. _____

3. _____

Name/Date _____

Elections 5

Call the local director of elections and ask them to be a guest speaker for the class. Look up that person's name and phone number and write it here.

_____
_____

U.S. Government Warm-ups: The Presidency

Name/Date _____

The Presidency 1

Fill in the blanks.

PRESIDENTIAL QUALIFICATIONS CHECKLIST:
I. QUALIFICATIONS: The candidate must be:
A. A natural-born citizen of the United States
B. At least 35 years of age, and
C. A resident of the U S at least 14 years.
US Constitution, Art. II, §1 (5)

To run for the presidency, a person must

be _____ years old, a

_____-born citizen,

and a resident of the United States for

_____ years.

Name/Date _____

The Presidency 2

Define *presidential veto*.

_____

_____

> *The final test of a leader is that he leaves behind him in other men the conviction and the will to carry on.*
> – Walter Lippmann

Name/Date _____

The Presidency 3

The official presidential song is:

_____

Name/Date _____

The Presidency 4

What is the address of the White House?

_____

Name/Date _____

The Presidency 5

Circle each of the following that are presidential landmarks.

1. Jefferson's home in Monticello
2. Mount Rushmore
3. The Washington Library
4. The John Adams Mountains
5. The John F. Kennedy Library

32

U.S. Government Warm-ups: The Presidency (cont.)

Name/Date _____

The Presidency 6

The 22nd amendment made it impossible for any president to be elected to more than two terms. Which president, in office during World War II, was the only one elected to four terms?

_____

Name/Date _____

The Presidency 7

A famous doctrine was written and issued in 1823 by this president who wanted the country to remain neutral during European conflicts. Who was he?

_____

Name/Date _____

The Presidency 8

Presidential powers are itemized under the "Executive Branch" article of what document?

_____

ARTICLE II, SECTION I

Name/Date _____

The Presidency 9

Match the paper money with the president appearing on the front side.

Grant	$2
McKinley	$5
Cleveland	$20
Jackson	$50
Jefferson	$500
Lincoln	$1,000

Name/Date _____

The Presidency 10

What presidential doctrine of 1947 enabled the government to provide funds to any country fighting Communism?

_____

U.S. Government Warm-ups: The Cabinet

The Cabinet 1

There are 15 executive department heads represented in the president's Cabinet today. On your own paper, name any 5 of the 15 departments.

The Cabinet 2

George Washington's Cabinet was made up of four department heads: Alexander Hamilton, Secretary of the Treasury; Gen. Henry Knox, Secretary of War; Edmund Randolph, Attorney General, and this man, the Secretary of State, who later became the third president.

Who was he? _____

The Cabinet 3

The Constitution provides that "the President can require the opinion in writing, of the principal officer in each of the executive departments, upon any subject relating to the duties of their respective office." Why is this important?

> *I not only use all the brains I have, but all I can borrow.*
> *– Woodrow Wilson*

_____

_____

_____

The Cabinet 4

On your own paper, describe how Cabinet secretaries are nominated today. Has it changed much since the founding of the country?

The Cabinet 5

What oath do Cabinet secretaries have to swear to? Look this up and write it on your own paper.

U.S. Government Warm-ups: The National Park Service

Name/Date _____

The National Park Service 1

President Woodrow Wilson signed legislation in 1916 that created the National Park Service. What features do you think a national park should have? Write your response on your own paper.

Name/Date _____

The National Park Service 2

What executive department is the National Park Service a part of?

_____

_____

_____

Name/Date _____

The National Park Service 3

Many of the nation's monuments are located in Washington, D.C. Read the clues to identify the monuments.

Every calling is great when greatly pursued.
– Oliver Wendell Holmes

1. An obelisk 555 feet high _____

2. A granite wall with thousands of names etched on it _____

3. A large cemetery for soldiers and the final resting place of President John F. Kennedy

_____

4. A sculpted figure of a president seated in a chair _____

Name/Date _____

The National Park Service 4

Many monuments and parks have been models for commemorative stamps. Design a new stamp featuring your favorite park or memorial on your own paper.

Name/Date _____

The National Park Service 5

What was the first national park? Who created it?

_____

_____

_____

_____

U.S. Government Warm-ups: Rules and Laws

Name/Date _____

Rules and Laws 1

There is a difference between a rule and a law.
Write "R" for rule and "L" for law.

_____ 1. Don't leave the fridge door open.

_____ 2. All drivers are required to have a license.

_____ 3. You may not run in the school building.

_____ 4. Stop for red traffic lights.

_____ 5. Follow highway speed limits.

> *People seldom improve when they have no other model but themselves to copy after.*
> — Oliver Goldsmith

Name/Date _____

Rules and Laws 2

You may not smoke in an elevator or in some public facilities. This is a rule that in some states has become a law. Why did people feel this was important enough to turn into a law? Use your own paper to explain.

Name/Date _____

Rules and Laws 3

Rule or Law? Circle the correct choice.

1. Homes must have smoke detectors.
   Rule or Law

2. Wait your turn in lines.
   Rule or Law

3. Don't waste paper.
   Rule or Law

Name/Date _____

Rules and Laws 4

Rule or Law? Circle the correct choice.

1. Get a license to go fishing.
   Rule or Law

2. Do not copy from someone's paper.
   Rule or Law

3. Do not steal from a store.
   Rule or Law

Name/Date _____

Rules and Laws 5

Think of a school rule that affects you. Is it fair? Why or why not? Explain on your own paper.

U.S. Government Warm-ups: Rules and Laws (cont.)

Name/Date _____

Rules and Laws 6

Laws made and passed by Congress or by state legislatures are called **statutes**. Using your own paper, give an example of a statute.

Name/Date _____

Rules and Laws 7

Laws passed by city governments are called **ordinances**. Using your own paper, give an example of an ordinance.

Name/Date _____

Rules and Laws 8

Fill in the blanks.

If someone is accused of breaking a statute or an ordinance, they are put on trial. A panel of peers, also called a _____, decides a person's guilt or innocence.

Name/Date _____

Rules and Laws 9

Jurors must be citizens who are not felons or _____ officers.

Name/Date _____

Rules and Laws 10

Without a system of rules, laws, and other means of keeping order, what might happen?

_____

_____

_____

Chronological Listing of Notable American Documents

1620	The Mayflower Compact	The first written agreement of self-government in America; the signers pledged to obey just and equal laws passed by the majority
1639	Fundamental Orders of Connecticut	The first written constitution in North America
1776	Virginia Declaration of Rights	Proclaimed the natural rights of men and the right to rebel against inadequate governments
1776	Declaration of Independence	Declared independence from the British government
1777	Articles of Confederation	Organized the first national government of the United States, officially approved in 1781
1783	Jay Treaty	Opposition to the capture of sailors on the high seas and the seizing of American ships
1787	Northwest Ordinance	States gave up any claims they had in the northwest to help open lands for American western settlements.
1788	The Constitution	Replaced the Articles of Confederation as the supreme law in the United States
1791	The Bill of Rights	First ten amendments to the Constitution
1793	Neutrality Proclamation	Issued by George Washington who stated, "This country will remain friendly and impartial toward belligerent warring powers."
1793	Fugitive Slave Law	Citizens of the North could be made to return runaway slaves to their owners.
1798	Sedition Act	A crime is committed if anyone publishes "any false, scandalous, and malicious" writing about the president, Congress, or the national government.
1823	The Monroe Doctrine	Said the United States would not take part in European affairs and would consider unfriendly any attempt by Europe to interfere in the Western Hemisphere.

Chronological Listing of Notable American Documents (cont.)

1860–61	Declaration of Causes	Gave reasons why Southern states were seceding from the Union.
1864	Emancipation Proclamation	All slaves in regions of rebellion against the United States were set free.
1917–18	Espionage Act	Made it a crime to interfere with the United States, speak out against the United States, or promote the success of its enemies during World War I
1937–39	Neutrality Acts	A series of laws barring the United States from any entanglement in foreign conflicts
1941	Atlantic Charter	Franklin Delano Roosevelt and Winston Churchill met to declare "four freedoms" for all: speech, worship, freedom from fear, and freedom from want.
1947	Truman Doctrine	Funds may be provided to aid countries resisting communist threats.
1949	North Atlantic Treaty	The nations of Europe and North America signed a pact against aggression from any country. American armed forces can be used to protect Western Europe.
1964	Civil Rights Act	Made racial discrimination in public places illegal and prohibited discrimination by employers on the basis of color, race, or national origin.
1965	Voting Rights Act	Outlawed discriminatory voting practices on the basis of race or color.
1968	Non-Proliferation of Nuclear Weapons	International safeguards were put into place for peaceful nuclear activities.
1973	War Powers Resolution	The president has the power to send armed forces into a hostile area indicated by circumstances but must inform Congress within 48 hours.
1991	Civil Rights Act	Discrimination is prohibited in voting, public schools, the workplace, or in any public facilities because of race, color, sex, religion, or national origin.

Colonial Government Graphic Organizer

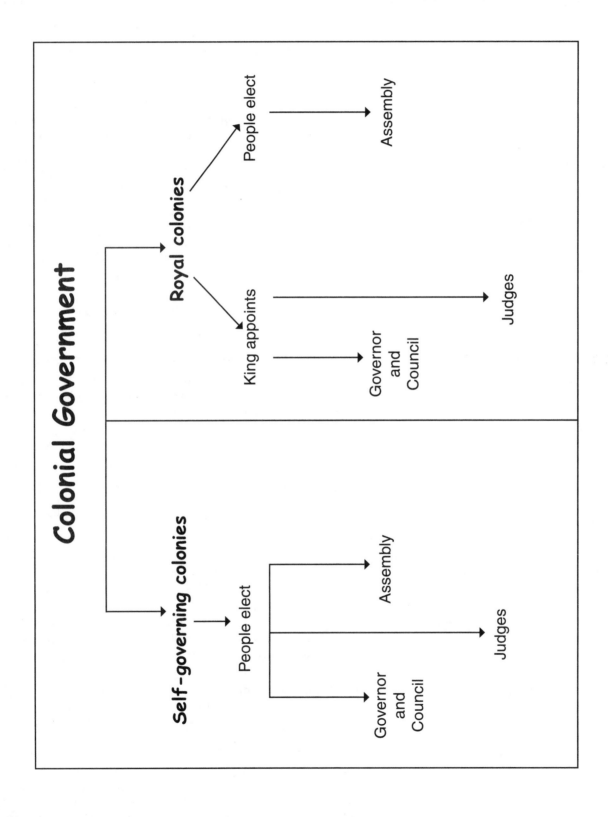

Colonial Government

Royal colonies

People elect → Assembly

King appoints → Governor and Council

→ Judges

Self-governing colonies

People elect → Assembly

→ Governor and Council

→ Judges

I Am an American

I am an American.
If you ask me what that means
I'll answer:

I love my country and my God;
I love my parents and they love me.
I respect my neighbors and deal with them fairly.
I am strong; I am happy; I am free.

I can speak without fear and act without shame,
And walk tall among the children of earth.
All the rights that I have I am willing to share.
I am proud of my nation—my birth.

I can work as I wish and play as I wish,
And think what I wish and say what I wish,
And do as I wish and pray as I wish,
So long as I'm decent and true.
My school is free and my church is free,
My country's laws are made for me,
And all in all it is good to be
An American.

I am glad that I am an American.
I am proud of my birthright, but humble, too.
And being an American
These things I must do:

I must speak the truth as I see the truth;
I must play by rules that are always fair.
I must not laugh at another's ways,
Or take more than is my share.

I must do no thing that will cause me shame.
I must walk tall and brave and free,
And I must help others to have
The rights that mean so much to me.

– Olive Burt, 1964

Answer Keys

The Mayflower Compact 1 (p. 2)
Answers will vary.

The Mayflower Compact 2 (p. 2)
To share in setting up a government, to enact just and equal laws, to promise to obey all laws, and to appoint officers.

The Mayflower Compact 3 (p. 2)
trading

The Mayflower Compact 4 (p. 2)
the Constitution and the Bill of Rights

The Mayflower Compact 5 (p. 2)
Answers will vary.

Colonial Government 1 (p. 3)
Burgesses, Jamestown, people

Colonial Government 2 (p. 3)
Farmers needed protection from the Indians and more representation in the House of Burgesses. Bacon acted against the king's appointed governor William Berkeley.

Colonial Government 3 (p. 3)
1. T   2. T   3. F

Colonial Government 4 (p. 3)
Rhode Island: religious freedom;
    separating church from state
New Jersey: religious freedom;
    a representative government
Pennsylvania: religious freedom;
    an elected assembly

Colonial Government 5 (p. 3)
Both have had their struggles to face and conquer. Examples: paying for government and public services, protecting the rights of citizens, immigration, etc.

Declaration of Independence 1 (p. 4)
events, people, political, connected

Declaration of Independence 2 (p. 4)
Answers will vary. Accept any five signers.

Declaration of Independence 3 (p. 4)
Answers will vary.

Declaration of Independence 4 (p. 4)
July 4th, 1776

Declaration of Independence 5 (p. 4)
Richard Henry Lee

Declaration of Independence 6 (p. 5)
A betrayal or breach of allegiance

Declaration of Independence 7 (p. 5)
Loyalists were loyal to England. Some were grateful to England for defeating the French in the French and Indian War, others were appointed to positions of power by the King, others were clergymen with the Church of England.

Declaration of Independence 8 (p. 5)
" . . . that all men are created equal, that they are endowed by their creator with certain unalienable rights, that among these are life, liberty, and the pursuit of happiness—"

Declaration of Independence 9 (p. 5)
These rights cannot be taken or given away.

Declaration of Independence 10 (p. 5)
Some of the grievances written into the Declaration include: Refusal of laws that would help the colonists govern themselves; forbade his governors to allow any laws without his permission and then neglected to bother with them; colonists should relinquish their right of representation in the legislature; prevented representatives from being elected; did not agree to the establishment of judiciary powers and made judges dependant on his will alone; sent officers to harass the people while using private homes for food and lodging; keeping soldiers in the colonies during peacetime; cutting off trade ties with other parts of the world; imposing taxes without consent of the colonists; depriving trial by jury and taking away charters and laws the colonists developed.

The Constitution 1 (p. 6)
Philadelphia, George Washington

The Constitution 2 (p. 6)
Pennsylvania

The Constitution 3 (p. 6)
The Bill of Rights

The Constitution 4–5 (p. 6)
Answers will vary.

The Constitution 6 (p. 7)
Note to the Teacher: Have a class contest to see who can memorize and recite the Preamble first.

The Constitution 7 (p. 7)
Tranquility: undisturbed, peaceful
Posterity: succeeding generations
Domestic: home, not foreign

The Constitution 8–9 (p. 7)
Answers will vary.

The Constitution 10 (p. 7)
Answers will vary, but should include that it is interpreted differently as times change, and it can be amended to make changes and continue to serve the people of the current age.

The Bill of Rights 1 (p. 8)
Constitution, 1791, amendments

The Bill of Rights 2 (p. 8)
religion, speech, press, assembly, petition

The Bill of Rights 3 (p. 8)
right to a speedy and public trial by jury; tried in the district where the crime occurrred; informed of the charges; can confront the witnesses against him; can obtain witnesses in his favor; can have the assistance of counsel

The Bill of Rights 4 (p. 8)
Answers will vary.

The Bill of Rights 5 (p. 8)
It can be changed, modified, and updated through the addition of amendments as the country and situations change.

The Bill of Rights 6 (p. 9)
All people should be treated fairly under the law regardless of their acts.

The Bill of Rights 7 (p. 9)
responsibilities

The Bill of Rights 8 (p. 9)
1. N   2. Y   3. Y   4. Y
5. N

The Bill of Rights 9 (p. 9)
Answers will vary.

The Bill of Rights 10 (p. 9)
1. a   2. c   3. d   4. b

A Bill Becomes a Law 1–2 (p. 10)
Answers will vary.

A Bill Becomes a Law 3 (p. 10)
1. 51 2. 218 3. 67   4. 288

A Bill Becomes a Law 4 (p. 10)
The House of Representatives, because originally the representatives were the only ones elected directly by the people.

A Bill Becomes a Law 5 (p. 10)
If the president does nothing with the bill for ten days and doesn't sign it and Congress is not in session, the bill dies.

Native Americans 1 (p. 11)
1. Y   2. Y   3. N   4. Y
5. N

Native Americans 2 (p. 11)
The Iroquois Confederacy (also known as the Iroquois League or the League of the Longhouse)

Native Americans 3 (p. 11)
The Bureau of Indian Affairs
Any two: administers and manages land held in trust by the United States for American Indians; leases land assets; directs agricultural programs; protects water and land rights; develops and maintains infrastructure and economic development; provides education to Native American students

Native Americans 4 (p. 11)
Answers will vary.

Native Americans 5 (p. 11)
He was a senator of mixed Northern Cheyenne ancestry from Colorado from 1993 to 2005.

Statehood 1 (p. 12)
western, Northwest Ordinance, states

Statehood 2 (p. 12)
1787, self-government

Statehood 3 (p. 12)
schools, would not

Statehood 4 (p. 12)
100 towns were settled

Statehood 5 (p. 12)
Answers will vary.

Statehood 6 (p. 13)
Answers will vary.

Statehood 7 (p. 13)
Hawaii (annexed 1898, state 1959), Texas (state 1845)

Statehood 8 (p. 13)
Answers will vary.

Statehood 9 (p. 13)
Virginia; West Virginia

Statehood 10 (p. 13)
49th and 50th

State and Local Governments 1 (p. 14)
5. all of the above

State and Local Governments 2 (p. 14)
three, executive, legislative, judicial

State and Local Governments 3 (p. 14)
governor, budget, answers will vary

State and Local Governments 4 (p. 14)
3. Constitution

State and Local Governments 5 (p. 14)
Answers will vary.

State and Local Governments 6 (p. 15)
4. all of the above

State and Local Governments 7 (p. 15)
4. all of the above

State and Local Governments 8 (p. 15)
Various state functions were efficient and similar from colony to colony. As the country expanded, new territories applying for statehood had a ready plan to follow. State constitutions vary a little, but follow the same general ideas.

State and Local Governments 9–10 (p. 15)
Answers will vary.

State and Local Governments 11–13 (p. 16)
Answers will vary.

State and Local Governments 14 (p. 16)
An elected board may deal with all these issues.

State and Local Governments 15 (p. 16)
Answers will vary.

State and Local Governments 16 (p. 17)
fire chief, police, health inspector

State and Local Governments 17 (p. 17)
highway patrol, Dept. of Motor Vehicles, forest ranger, fire marshal, also health inspector

State and Local Governments 18 (p. 17)
IRS, Food and Drug Administration, Dept. of Agriculture, FBI

State and Local Governments 19 (p. 17)
911

State and Local Governments 20 (p. 17)
Answers will vary.

Women in Government 1 (p. 18)
Ruth Bader Ginsburg

Women in Government 2 (p. 18)
Medal of Honor

Women in Government 3 (p. 18)
Italy

Women in Government 4 (p. 18)
Answers will vary.

Women in Government 5 (p. 18)
1. Secretary of Labor
2. Secretary of Heath, Education, and Welfare
3. Secretary of Housing and Urban Development, Secretary of Health and Human Services
4. Secretary of Transportation, Secretary of Labor
5. Secretary of Energy
6. Attorney General
7. Secretary of State
8. Secretary of State
9. Secretary of Labor

Women in Government 6 (p. 19)
1. Dix exposed the poor conditions in mental health facilities, pushing the state legislature in Massachusetts to pass laws to improve them.
2. Barton was the first woman to clerk in the government patent office and later became the founder and first president of the American Red Cross.
3. Mott spoke out against slavery, using her home as a station for the Underground Railroad, and she later formed women's suffrage groups favoring social, political, and economic equality.

Women in Government 7 (p. 19)
Answers will vary.

Women in Government 8 (p. 19)
Carrie Nation

Women in Government 9 (p. 19)
Eleanor Roosevelt

Women in Government 10 (p. 19)
Answers will vary.

Minorities in Government 1 (p. 20)
1. Blanche K. Bruce
2. Jeannette Rankin
3. Shirley Chisholm
4. Daniel K. Inouye
5. Thurgood Marshall
6. Carol Mosley-Braun
7. Ezequiel Cabeza de Baca (New Mexico, 1917)

Minorities in Government 2 (p. 20)
Colin Powell

Minorities in Government 3 (p. 20)
Hillary Clinton, Barack Obama

Minorities in Government 4 (p. 20)
Condoleezza Rice

Minorities in Government 5 (p. 20)
U.S. Surgeon General

Government Agencies 1 (p. 21)
Answers will vary.

Government Agencies 2 (p. 21)
It assures that food is safe and wholesome and that cosmetics, medical devices, and drugs are safe and will do no harm.

Government Agencies 3 (p. 21)
Langley, Virginia

Government Agencies 4 (p. 21)
Be a U.S. citizen, be at least 23 years old, pass a vision test, and others.

Government Agencies 5 (p. 21)
Treasury Department

Government Agencies 6 (p. 22)
injured, families

Government Agencies 7 (p. 22)
natural: forces of nature, such as hurricanes, tornadoes, or floods.
man-made: terrorist attacks, chemical warfare, biological warfare, explosive devices

Government Agencies 8 (p. 22)
2, 4, and 6 should be circled.

Government Agencies 9–10 (p. 22)
Answers will vary.

Military Branches of the Government 1 (p. 23)
1. Answers will vary.
2. The President
3. Secretary of Defense
4. the Army, Navy, Marine Corps, Air Force, and Coast Guard

Military Branches of the Government 2 (p. 23)
1. T   2. F   3. F   4. F

Military Branches of the Government 3 (p. 23)
to fight the Revolutionary War

Military Branches of the Government 4 (p. 23)
The ROTC trains students for leadership roles in the Armed Forces. To qualify for the ROTC, you must be a U.S. citizen between the ages of 17 and 26, have a high school diploma or GED with a 2.5 GPA and a 920 on the SAT or a 19 on the ACT, meet certain physical standards, and agree to serve the military after schooling.

Military Branches of the Government 5 (p. 23)
Medal of Honor: heroism beyond
    the call of duty
Distinguished Service Cross:
    extraordinary heroism
Silver Star: gallantry in action

The United States Mint 1 (p. 24)
Coinage

The United States Mint 2 (p. 24)
In any order: 1¢, 5¢, 10¢, 25¢, 50¢, and $1.00

The United States Mint 3 (p. 24)
Philadelphia, PA, and Denver, CO

The United States Mint 4 (p. 24)
Answers will be based on market value.

The United States Mint 5 (p. 24)
Have students share their responses.

Immigration 1 (p. 25)
Ellis Island

Immigration 2 (p. 25)
c/d, d/c, b, e, a

Immigration 3 (p. 25)
1800s, increased, closed

Immigration 4 (p. 25)
Immigration quotas expanded to 350,000.

Immigration 5 (p. 25)
A quota is a set limit or number.

Immigration 6 (p. 26)
legal: based in or sanctioned by a
    law
illegal: not sanctioned or based by
    law; against the law

Immigration 7 (p. 26)
U.S. Citizenship and Immigration Services

Immigration 8 (p. 26)
Answers will vary.

Immigration 9 (p. 26)
naturalization: the process by
    which an immigrant becomes a
    citizen

Immigration 10 (p. 26)
1. primarily European countries
    and China
2. All countries
3. Answers will vary.

Immigration 11 (p. 27)
passport: a license empowering
    personal travel out of a
    country
visa: a temporary permit for entry
    into a country

Immigration 12 (p. 27)
Ellis Island and Angel Island

Immigration 13 (p. 27)
Yes. You would be a foreign-born citizen.

Immigration 14–15 (p. 27)
Answers will vary.

The NARA 1 (p. 28)
This generally includes the records of a country, family, or organization.

The NARA 2 (p. 28)
Congress, documents,
U.S. Government

The NARA 3 (p. 28)
1. Declaration of Independence
2. Bill of Rights
3. Emancipation Proclamation
4. Constitution

The NARA 4 (p. 28)
1. Y   2. N   3. Y   4. Y
5. N

The NARA 5 (p. 28)
Any citizen has the right and the opportunity to see or read the material.

The Census Bureau 1 (p. 29)
U.S. Constitution, ten, representatives, state, 2010

The Census Bureau 2 (p. 29)
A period of time spanning ten years.

The Census Bureau 3 (p. 29)
1. Y   2. N   3. Y   4. N

The Census Bureau 4 (p. 29)
1. schools
2. transportation
3. social services

The Census Bureau 5 (p. 29)
Answers will vary.

The Electoral College 1 (p. 30)
1. T   2. T   3. F

The Electoral College 2 (p. 30)
Members from each political party are called "electors." They pledge themselves before an election to vote for the party's candidate.

The Electoral College 3 (p. 30)
270 votes

The Electoral College 4 (p. 30)
1 and 2 should be circled.

The Electoral College 5 (p. 30)
There are 538 electoral votes; 435, representing one for each member of the House of Representatives, 100, representing each member of the Senate, and 3 for the District of Columbia. Larger states have more votes because of larger populations.

Elections 1 (p. 31)
polling/voting, candidates, electoral

Elections 2 (p. 31)
15th (1870): No citizen should lose the right to vote because of race, color, or because they were formerly a slave.
19th (1920): No citizen shall be refused the right to vote because of being a woman.
24th (1964): No citizen shall be prevented from voting for a president, vice-president, senator, or representative because they are unable to pay a poll tax.
26th (1971): No citizen 18 years or older should be denied the right to vote because of age.

Elections 3 (p. 31)
Check marks should be by 1, 3, and 5.

Elections 4 (p. 31)
Answers will vary.

Elections 5 (p. 31)
Answers will vary. This could be a meaningful experience for students.

The Presidency 1 (p. 32)
35, natural, 14

The Presidency 2 (p. 32)
a refusal to approve a bill passed by Congress

The Presidency 3 (p. 32)
"Hail to the Chief"

The Presidency 4 (p 32)
1600 Pennsylvania Avenue, Washington, D.C.

The Presidency 5 (p. 32)
1, 2, and 5 should be circled.

The Presidency 6 (p. 33)
Franklin D. Roosevelt

The Presidency 7 (p. 33)
James Monroe

The Presidency 8 (p. 33)
the U.S. Constitution

The Presidency 9 (p. 33)

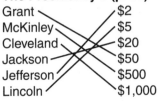

Grant — $50
McKinley — $500
Cleveland — $1,000
Jackson — $20
Jefferson — $2
Lincoln — $5

The Presidency 10 (p. 33)
the Truman Doctrine

The Cabinet 1 (p. 34)
Any five of the following: Treasury, Agriculture, Commerce, Homeland Security, State, Defense, Education, Energy, Health and Human Services, Housing and Urban Development, Interior, Labor, Transportation, Veteran Affairs, Justice

The Cabinet 2 (p. 34)
Thomas Jefferson

The Cabinet 3 (p. 34)
The president can keep current and stay knowledgeable about all department activities by getting advice and information from people who are focused on those areas.

The Cabinet 4 (p. 34)
They are nominated by the president and confirmed or rejected by the Senate.

The Cabinet 5 (p. 34)
I _____, do solemnly swear (or affirm) that I will support and defend the Constitution of the United States against all enemies, foreign and domestic; that I will bear true faith and allegiance to the same; that I take this obligation freely without any mental reservation or purpose of evasion; and that I will well and faithfully discharge the duties of the office on which I am about to enter. So help me God.

The National Park Service 1 (p. 35)
Answers will vary.

The National Park Service 2 (p. 35)
the Department of the Interior

The National Park Service 3 (p. 35)
1. Washington Monument
2. Vietnam War Memorial
3. Arlington National Cemetery
4. Lincoln Memorial

The National Park Service 4 (p. 35)
Designs will vary.

The National Park Service 5 (p. 35)
Yellowstone National Park was created by Congress in 1872.

Rules and Laws 1 (p. 36)
1. R   2. L   3. R   4. L
5. L

Rules and Laws 2 (p. 36)
Answers will vary.

Rules and Laws 3 (p. 36)
1. Law   2. Rule   3. Rule

Rules and Laws 4 (p. 36)
1. Law   2. Rule   3. Law

Rules and Laws 5 (p. 36)
Answers will vary.

Rules and Laws 6–7 (p. 37)
Answers will vary.

Rules and Laws 8 (p. 37)
jury

Rules and Laws 9 (p. 37)
police

Rules and Laws 10 (p. 37)
Answers will vary.